# The Rhythm Lab's Exhibition Duets For Drum Set

*Contemporary Studies for Traditional Drum Set*

By Bermudian author and professor

## Eddie Ming

*Second Edition*

ISBN Number: 978-0-9569878-1-5

Copyright © 2011  Eddie Ming

International Copyright Secured
All Rights Reserved
No part of this publication may be reproduced in any form
or by any means
without the prior written permission of the publisher.

Published by: Eddie Ming Publishing
*Mailing address of the publisher:*
Eddie Ming's Rhythm Lab, # 9 – 39 Cut Road, St. George's  GE 04,  B E R M U D A
*Fax:*  441-297-4361
*E-mail:  emingflatride@btcnet.bm*
*Or,  eddiemingflatride@gmail.com*

Printed by CreateSpace

**Available from Amazon.com**
&
The Rhythm Lab – BERMUDA
&
Eddie Ming's Drum School, Bermuda.

# *El Laboratorio del Ritmo*
# *Exposición Dúos para Batería*

*Estudios Contemporáneos*

*por El Grupo de Percusión Tradicional*

Por el autor y profesor de Las Bermudas

## Eddie Ming

*Segunda Edición*

**Número de ISBN: 978-0-9569878-1-5**

**Copyright © 2011   Eddie Ming**

**Derecho de autor Internacional Aseguró**
**Todos los derechos reservados**
Bien no reservó parte de esta publicación puede ser reproducida en nínguna forma,
ni por ningún medio sin el permiso escrito previo del Editor.

*Publicado por:* La Editorial Eddie Ming
*Dirección de envoi del editor:*
Eddie Ming's Rhythm Lab, #9 – 39 Cut Road, St. George's  GE 04, Las BERMUDAS
Fax:  441-297-4361
Dirección por correo electrónico:
*emingflatride@btcnet.bm   o,   eddiemingflatride@gmail.com*

Impreso por CreateSpace

**Disponible en Amazon.com**
*y*
El Laboratorio Del Ritmo – Las BERMUDAS
*y,*
La Escuela de Batería de Eddie Ming, Las Bermudas

# Contents

| | |
|---|---|
| About The Author | Page 3 |
| Eddie's Methodology | Pages 4, 5. 6, 7, 8, 9, 10 |
| Certificates | |
| Acknowledgements | Pages 11, 12 |
| Introduction | Pages 13, 14 |
| Notes | Pages 15, 16, 17 |
| Notation Key - Clave de la Notación | Page 18 |

## 14 Musical Duets:-

| | |
|---|---|
| Duet A #1 & A #2 | Pages 19 & 20 |
| Duet B #1 & B #2 | Pages 21, 22 |
| Duet C #1 & C #2 | Pages 23, 24 |
| Duet D #1 & D #2 | Pages 25, 26 |
| Duet E #1 & E #2 | Pages 27, 28 |
| Duet F #1 & F #2 | Pages 29, 30 |
| Duet G #1 & G #2 | Pages 31, 32 |
| Duet H #1 & H #2 | Pages 33. 34 |
| Duet I #1 & I #2 | Pages 35, 36 |
| Duet J #1 & J #2 | Pages 37, 38 |
| Duet K #1 & K #2 | Pages 39, 40 |
| Duet L #1 & L #2 | Pages 41, 42 |
| Duet M #1 & M #2 | Pages 43, 44, 45, 46 |
| Duet N #1 & N #2 | Pages 47, 48, 49, 50 |
| Illustrations | Pages 51, 52, 53, 54, 55 |
| Orchestrating Ideas | Page 56, 57 |
| Hi-Hat Procedure | Page 59 |
| Additional Open & Close Hi-Hat Patterns with Added Bass and Snare Drum Notes | Page 60 |
| Illustrations continued | Page 61 |
| History of Sabian Cymbal Makers | Pages 62, 63 |
| **38 Bonus Solo Ideas** | **Page 64** |
| Additional Bonus Groove Ideas | Page 65 |
| Bonus Section A1 | Page 66 |
| Bonus Section B1 | Page 67 |
| Bonus Section C1 | Page 68 |
| Bonus Section A2 | Page 69 |
| Bonus Section B2 | Pages 70, 71 |
| Bonus Grooves C2 | Pages 72, 73 |
| Bonus Grooves D2 | Page 74 |
| Bonus Grooves E2 | Page 75 |
| 6/8 Bonus Grooves | Pages 76, 77 |
| Essential Snare Drum Exercises A & B | Pages 78, 79, 80, 81, 82 |
| Jazz Studies | Page 83 |
| 4/4 Jazz Studies: J1 | Pages 84, 85 |
| J2 | Pages 86, 87 |
| J3 | Page 88 |
| Ride Cymbal Variations | Page 89 |
| 3/4 Jazz Studies: J4 | Pages 90, 91 |
| J5 | Pages 92, 93 |
| J6 | Pages 94, 95. |
| Shifting Time Signatures with Open & Closed Hi-Hat Ideas | Pages 96, 97, 98 |
| Jazz Phrases for Brushes | Page 99 |
| Eddie at KoSa 2010 | Page 100 |
| Dedication | Page 101 |
| History of La Escuela Nacional de Música | Pages 103, 104 |
| Book Review | Page 105 |
| Schools in Cuba where Prof. Eddie Ming has taught | Page 106 |

# Contenidos

| | |
|---|---|
| *Sobre el autor* | *Página 3* |
| *Certificados de la Metodología de Eddie* | *Páginas 4, 5, 6, 7, 8, 9, 10* |
| *Agradecimientos* | *Páginas 11, 12* |
| *Introducción* | *Páginas 13, 14* |
| *Anotación* | *Páginas 15, 16, 17* |
| *Clave De La Notación* | *Página 18* |

## 14 Dúos Musicales:-

| | |
|---|---|
| *Dúo A #1 y A #2* | *Páginas 19, 20* |
| *Dúo B #1 y B #2* | *Páginas 11, 12, y 22* |
| *Dúo C #1 y C #2* | *Páginas 23, 24* |
| *Dúo D #1 y D #2* | *Páginas 25, 26* |
| *Dúo E #1 y E #2* | *Páginas 27, 28* |
| *Dúo F #1 y F #2* | *Páginas 29, 30* |
| *Dúo G #1 y G #2* | *Páginas 31, 32* |
| *Dúo H #1 y H #2* | *Páginas 33, 34* |
| *Dúo I #1 y I #2* | *Páginas 35, 36* |
| *Dúo J #1 y J #2* | *Páginas 37, 38* |
| *Dúo K #1 y K#2* | *Páginas 39, 40* |
| *Dúo L #1 y L #2* | *Páginas 41, 42* |
| *Dúo M#1 y M #2* | *Páginas 43, 44, 45, 46* |
| *Dúo N #1 y N #2* | *Páginas 47, 48, 49, 50* |
| *Ilustraciónes* | *Páginas 51, 52, 53, 54, 55* |
| *Ideas Orquestrales* | *Páginas 56, 57* |
| *Procedimiento de Platillos Hi-Hat* | *Página 59* |
| *Patrones Adicionales de Hi-Hat Cerrados y Abiertos* | *Página 60* |
| *Historia de los platillos Sabian* | *Páginas 62, 63* |
| **38 Ideas Extras de Solos** | **Página 64** |
| *Ideas Adicionales de Groove* | *Página 65* |
| *Sección Extra A1* | *Página 66* |
| *Sección Extra B1* | *Página 67* |
| *Sección Extra C1* | *Página 68* |
| *Grooves Extras A2* | *Página 69* |
| *Grooves Extras B2* | *Páginas 70, 71* |
| *Grooves Extras **C2*** | *Páginas 72, 73* |
| *Grooves Extras D2* | *Página 74* |
| *Grooves Extras E2* | *Página 75* |
| *Grooves Extras 6/8* | *Páginas 76, 77* |
| *Ejercicios Esenciales de Caja* | *Página 78* |
| *Estudios Adicionales que incluyen Ejercicios de Caja Esenciales (p A y B)* | *Páginas 79, 80, 81, 82* |
| *Estudios de Jazz* | *Página 83* |
| *Estudios de Jazz 4/4 p J1* | *Páginas 84, 85* |
| *Estudios de Jazz 4/4 p J2* | *Páginas 86, 87* |
| *Estudios de Jazz 4/4 p J3* | *Página 88* |
| *Variaciones de Címbalos* | *Página 89* |
| *Estudios de Jazz 3/4 p J4* | *Páginas 90, 91* |
| *Estudios de Jazz 3/4 p J5* | *Páginas 92, 93* |
| *Estudios de Jazz 3/4 p J6* | *Páginas 94, 95* |
| *Cambiando el Compás con Ideas Sobre Platillos Hi-Hat Abiertos y Cerrados* | *Página 96* |
| *Ideas Adicionales para Cambiar El Compás con Hi-Hat Abierto y Cerrado* | *Páginas 97, 98* |
| *Frases de Jazz para Escobillas* | *Página 99* |
| *Eddie en KoSa en 2010* | *Página 100* |
| *Dedicación* | *Página 101* |
| *Historia de la Escuela Nacional* | *Páginas 103, 104* |
| *Reseña del Libro* | *Página 105* |
| *Escuelas en Cuba donde el Prof. Eddie Ming ha enseñado* | *Página 106* |

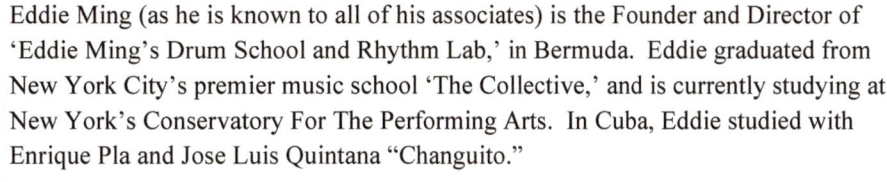

Eddie Ming (as he is known to all of his associates) is the Founder and Director of 'Eddie Ming's Drum School and Rhythm Lab,' in Bermuda. Eddie graduated from New York City's premier music school 'The Collective,' and is currently studying at New York's Conservatory For The Performing Arts. In Cuba, Eddie studied with Enrique Pla and Jose Luis Quintana "Changuito."

Eddie started teaching at the Escuela Nacional de Música in Cuba in 2008, and in 2009, he produced and conducted 'An Afternoon of Percussion – Traditional and Latin Jazz,' which was held at Havana's 'Casa de la Cultura de la Plaza.' The concert featured students from Bermuda and Cuba. The main objective of this joint venture, was to bring the two islands and their cultures together through music. Since then, he continues to teach at the Escuela Nacional de Música; the Escuela Elemental de Música Alejandro Garcia Caturla; and the Instituto Superior de Arte (ISA). Eddie produces an annual recital in Havana, hosted by SABIAN Cymbal Makers of New Brunswick, Canada.

In August 2002, Eddie became a Sabian Factory Trained Associate.

In 2007, he received a Founder's Award from The Bermuda Arts Council.

In July 2010, Professor Eddie Ming was presented with a Life-Time Achievement Award by Montreal's KoSa International Percussion Academy 'for his tireless dedication and devotion to musical education, and the promotion of young talent in Bermuda.'

## *Sobre El Autor Ernest Edward Ming*

*Eddie Ming (como es reconocido por todos sus asociados) es el Fundador y el Director de La Escuela de Batería de Eddie Ming y Laboratorio de Ritmo, en Bermuda. Eddie se graduó de la escuela primera de música de Ciudad de Nueva York 'El Colectivo,' y estudia actualmente en El Conservatorio de Nueva York Para Las Artes Interpretativas. En Cuba, Eddie estudió con Enrique Pla y Jose Luis Quintana "Changuito."*

*Eddie empezó a enseñar en La Escuela Nacional de Música en Cuba en 2008; y en 2009, produjo y realizó 'Una Tarde de Percusión (An Afternoon Of Percussion) – Jazz Tradicional y Latino,' que se tuvo lugar en La Habana, en 'La Casa de la Cultura de la Plaza.' El concierto presentó a estudiantes de Bermuda y Cuba. El principal objetivo de esta empresa conjunta, fue de reunir las dos islas y sus culturas por un solo objetivo, la música. Desde entonces, el continúa a enseñar en La Escuela Nacional de Música; y en La Escuela Elemental de Música Alejandro Garcia Caturla; y en El Instituto Superior de Arte (ISA); Eddie produce un recital anual en La Habana, acogido por los Fabricantes de Címbalo de SABIAN de Nuevo Brunswick, Canadá.*

*En agosto 2002, Eddie se convirtió en asociado de la Fábrica de SABIAN.*

*En 2007, recibió el Premio de Fundador del Concilio de Artes de Bermuda.*

*En Julio de 2010, la Kosa Academia Internacional de Percusión de Montreal presentó un premio de vida al profesor Eddie Ming 'por su dedicación musical, y la promoción de los jóvenes talentos en las Bermudas.'*

In the name of

# Her Majesty
# Queen Elizabeth the Second

This Certificate of Honour
is awarded to

*Professor Eddie Ming*

of *St. George's Parish*

in recognition of valuable services given to Her Majesty

*for his service to the world of music*

Date *31st December 2008*

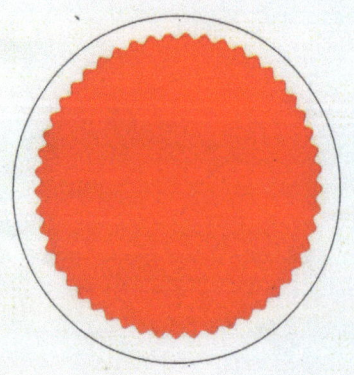

Governor and Commander-in-Chief

Havana, December 19, 2011

To whom it may concern,

Eddie Ming´s figure comes to me as that one of a cultivator of music. He is a person who goes to every corner of the world giving away his knowledge willingly to share it with the youngest.

His presence in Cuba has been received with love by many percussion specialists who have shown appreciation for his contribution of unquestionable values.

Every Cuban youngster who gets in contact with the book of drums set studies by Eddie Ming will receive his teachings and will be grateful forever.

I deeply appreciate Professor Ming for the book and everything that it means for us.

Prof. Roberto Chorens Dotres
Principal of Conservatory "Amadeo Roldán"

February 2, 2010

Eddie Ming's Drum School &
Rhythm Lab
# 9 -39 Cut Road
St. George's GE 04
Bermuda

Attention: Professor Eddie Ming

Dear Eddie:

We at SABIAN wish to congratulate you on your new diploma and all the fine work you've done for us and for music in Cuba.

Your fine work does indeed coincide with all our efforts to spread the value of music there.

Best Regards from us all,
SABIAN

Robert Zildjian

*THE NATIONAL CENTER OF ARTS SCHOOLS OF CUBA awards the present acknowledgement to:*

*<u>ERNEST EDWARD MING</u>, professor of percussion from Bermudas for:*

*His valuable contribution to the Methodology of teaching Traditional Drums at the Conservatory "Amadeo Roldán" in May 2008*

*So that this may be officially recorded and in witness whereof, the undersigned hereto set their hand in Havana, Cuba on the eighteenth day of December, 2010*

Rolando Ortega Álvarez
Director

THE NATIONAL CENTER OF ARTS SCHOOLS OF CUBA awards the present acknowledgement to:

**ERNEST EDWARD MING**, professor of percussion from Bermudas for:

Creating a Cultural Exchange Program between the Escuela Nacional de Música de Cuba and Eddie Ming's Rhythm Lab, Bermuda in 2008

So that this may be officially recorded and in witness whereof, the undersigned hereto set their hand in Havana, Cuba on the eighteenth day of December, 2010

Rolando Ortega Álvarez
Director

THE NATIONAL CENTER OF ARTS SCHOOLS OF CUBA awards the present acknowledgement to:

**ERNEST EDWARD MING**, professor of percussion from Bermudas for:

His valuable contribution to the Methodology of teaching Traditional Drums at the Elementary Music School " Alejandro García Caturla," in 2009

So that this may be officially recorded and in witness whereof, the undersigned hereto set their hand in Havana, Cuba on the eighteenth day of December, 2010

Rolando Ortega Álvarez
Director

THE NATIONAL CENTER OF ARTS SCHOOLS OF CUBA awards the present acknowledgement to:

ERNEST EDWARD MING, professor of percussion from Bermudas for:

His valuable contribution to the Methodology of teaching Traditional Drums at CNART, in December 2010

So that this may be officially recorded and in witness whereof, the undersigned hereto set their hand in Havana, Cuba on the eighteenth day of December, 2010

Rolando Ortega Alvarez
Director

# ACKNOWLEDGEMENTS

**Eddie would like to extend his sincere appreciation to the following people from the Rhythm Lab's workshop :**

**To:**

**Bryson Doers, Tajai O'Connor, Alfred Nick Swan, Gracie Edwards and Stephanie Howes, for reviewing this text before going to print.**

**Performing at Casa de la Cultura de la Plaza: Tajai, Gracie, Stephanie, Nick & Bryson, Havana 2009**

**We, in Cuba, and in Bermuda, would like to personally thank the Chief Executive Officer, Robert Zildjian, and SABIAN, for their fine selection of cymbals for our annual concert – 'An Afternoon of Percussion and Jazz.' Our love for SABIAN Cymbal Makers will endure. Also, I would like to mention that SABIAN's most innovative, modern, dark cymbals, HHX, were the cymbals that were most in demand by international drummers and Cuban percussionists alike, for Havana's 2009 International Jazz Festival.**

**Eddie would like to thank these four drummers in Bermuda: Sheldon Bean, Howie Rego, Andy Newmark, and Ronnie Lopes, who took the time out to share ideas with him early in his development.**

# *AGRADECIMIENTOS*

Eddie wishes to thank the following people

for their kind assistance with the Spanish translations of this text :

*Eddie desea agradecer a las siguientes personas*

*por su amable ayuda con los traducciones al español de este texto:*

Aldo Mazza

Profesor Sonia Salas

Profesor Alejandro Vázquez

Profesor Alexis Sánchez

Wendy Ming

Tanya Walker

Silvia Rodríguez

El señor Vicente Pouso Martín

# INTRODUCTION

This text was written to make available a new approach to musical duets for drumset from the author's 'Rhythm Lab.'

Traditional duets were written for two snare drums that provided the student with the material needed for the development of reading and ensemble skills – the principles of which are very much the same as for drumset duets. They will also expose the student to different Funk, Rhythm and Blues, and Rock idioms; and capture the essence of these working beats that are musical, and which can often directly apply to actual music-making situations.

### **Practice Tips:**

Both parts of each duet should be learnt in order to become aware of what the other drummer is doing; and to develop a better sense of rhythm between each other to make the duet complete.

### **Sticking:**

The Sticking will be left up to the individual to decide what works best for smooth execution of the fills.

The use of the metronome would be advisable

Remember to start slowly, and to increase the tempo when you are more familiar with the material given.

The key to developing and perfecting this particular style, is to continue to review each duet throughout this text.

# INTRODUCCIÓN

*Este texto fue escrito para poner a disposición un nuevo enfoque de duetos musicales de ritmo de batería por el laboratorio del autor.*

*Duetos tradicionales fueron escritas por dos tambores de la trampa que proporcionan al alumno con el material necesario para el desarrollo de habilidades de lectura y conjunto – los principios de que son muy parecido a los de dúos batería. También expondrá al estudiante a diferentes Funk, Rhythm and Blues, Rock y modismos, y capturer la esencia de estos ritmos de trabajo que son musicales, y que a menudo se puede aplicar directamente a las situaciones reales de hacer música.*

### *Consejos para la práctica:*

*Ambas partes de cada dúo se debe aprender, a fin de tomar conciencia de lo que el otro está*

*haciendo el baterista, y para desarrollar un mejor sentido del ritmo entre unos y otros para hacer el dueto completa.*

### *Piquetes*:

*El baqueteo se deja en manos del individuo para decidir qué funciona mejor para la buena ejecución de los rellenos y combinaciones de manos.*

*El uso del metrónomo es aconsejable.*

*Se debe comenzar lentamente y aumentar el ritmo cuando usted está más familiarizado con el material dado. La clave para el desarrollo y perfeccionamiento de este estilo particular, es que siga examinando cada dúo lo largo de este texto.*

**Professor Eddie Ming with student, Tatiana Torres, Conservatory Amadeo Roldan, 2010**

**Professor Eddie Ming with student, Mary Karla Garcia, Conservatory Amadeo Roldan, 2010**

# Presented here, is a list of terms used in this text:

**REPEAT SIGNS**
Play the measure within the repeat signs

**REPEAT MEASURE SIGN**
Repeat the preceding measure

**REPEAT MEASURE SIGN**
Repeat the number of preceding measures indicated

**CONTINUE TO KEEP THE TIME GOING**

**ACCENTED NOTE**

**ABBREVIATIONS/SYMBOLS:**

**CB** = CYMBAL BELL         **SD** = SNARE DRUM

**RC** = RIDE CYMBAL         **FT** = FLOOR TOM

**HH** = HI-HAT              **BD** = BASS DRUM

**TT** = TOM TOM

"Fingering" in connection with drumming, refers to the Right and Left Hand strokes, such as R R L L, R L R R, etc.

# Se presenta aquí una lista de términos utilizados en este texto:

**LOS SIGNOS DE REPETICIÓN**
*Tocar los compases dentro de los signos de repetición*

**EL SIGNO DE REPETICIÓN**
*Repita el compás anterior*

**EL SIGNO DE REPETICIÓN**
*Repita el número indicado de compases anteriores*

**SIGA MANTENIENDO EL TIEMPO**           / / / /

**UNA NOTA ACENTUADA**                   >

**ABREVIATURAS/SÍMBOLOS:**

**CB** = *LA COPA DE PLATILLO*           **SD** = *CAJA*

**RC** = *PLATILLO "RIDE"*               **FD** = *TOM TOM DE PIE*

**HH** = *PLATILLOS CERRADO (HI-HAT)*    **BD** = *BOMBO*

**TT** = *TOM TOM DE AIRE*

"Dedos" en relación con tambores, se refiere a la derecha y golpes de la mano izquierda como  D D I I,  D I D D,  etc.

# Notation Key
## Clave de la Notación

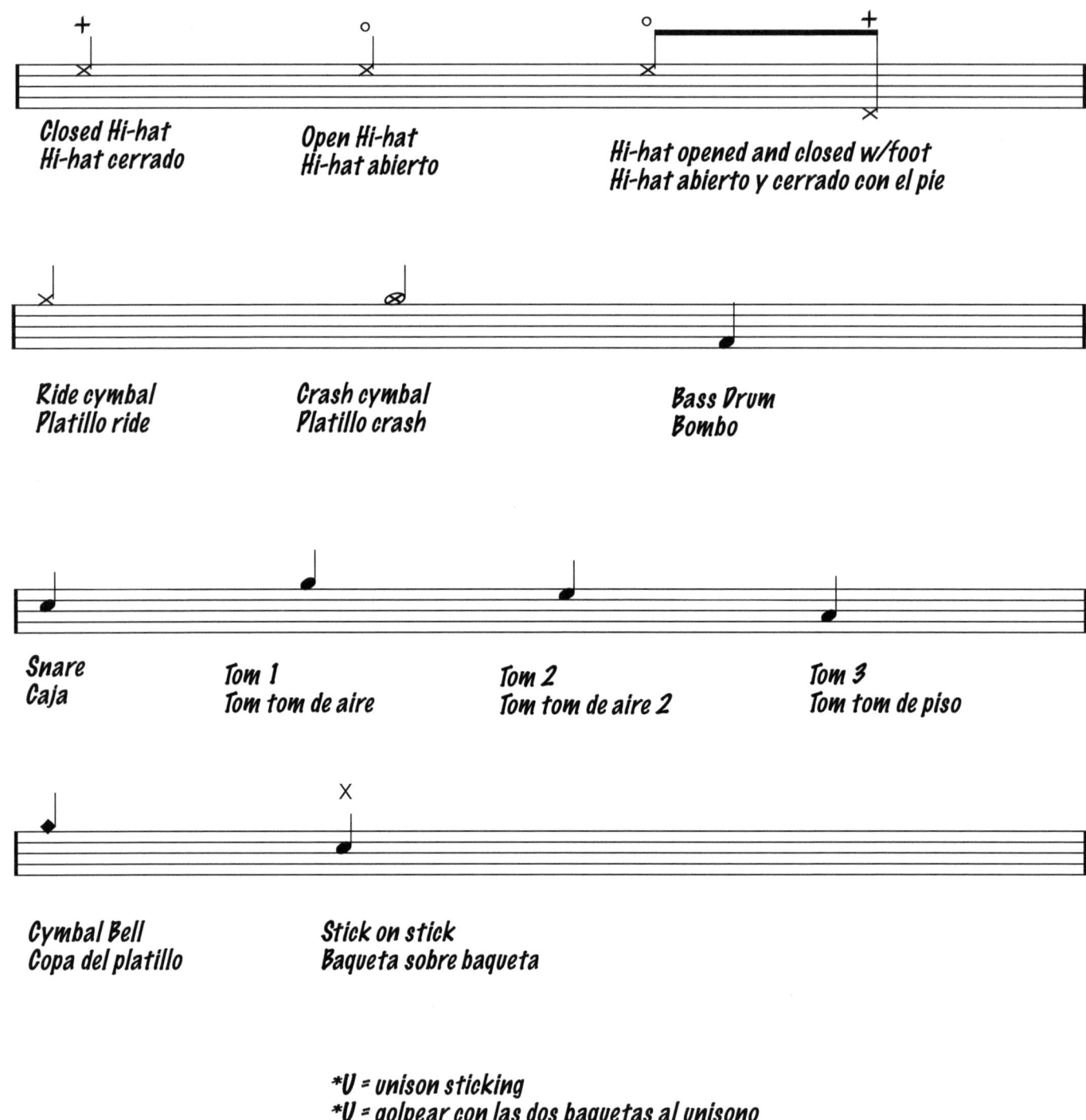

# Duet A
## Drums #1

# Duet A
## Drums #2

# Duet B
## Drums #1

# Duet B
## Drums #2

# Duet C
## Drums #1

# Duet C
## Drums #2

# Duet D
## Drums #1

# Duet D
## Drums #2

# Duet E
## Drums #1

# Duet E
## Drums #2

# Duet F
## Drums #1

29

# Duet F
## Drums #2

# Duet G
## Drums #1

# Duet G
## Drums #2

# Duet H
## Drums #1

# Duet H
## Drums #2

# Duet 1
## Drums #1

# Duet I
## Drums #2

# Duet J
## Drums #1

# Duet J
## Drums #2

# Duet K
## Drums #1

# Duet K
## Drums #2

# Duet L
## Drums #1

# Duet L
## Drums #2

# Duet M
## Drums #1

43

# Duet M
## Drums #2

# Duet N
## Drums #1

# Duet N
## Drums #2

# Beat goes on for Prof. Ming!

by Alex Scrymgeour

Bermudian percussionist and music teacher Professor Eddie Ming with students who took part in his workshops held this summer at the Cuban National Centre School for the Performing Arts in Havana and *(below)* presiding at the Havana concert put on by his Bermudian and Cuban students

Eddie's first, 'Annual Afternoon of Percussion and Jazz,' 2009, certificate presentation.
Pictured, is Bermudian Jazz student, Alfred Nick Swan receiving his certificate from Cuban director, Amalia Garcia, while shaking hands, and having a bit of a joke. (Many thanks for telling the story about what 'The Rhythm Lab' means to the Bermudian people who attended a very musical recital, which was held at the Casa De La Cultura De La Plaza, and sponsored by SABIAN Cymbal Makers of Canada).

## HAVANA GREAT TIME IN CUBA . . .

Bermudian percussionist and professor Eddie Ming is pictured with students who took part in his workshops during the summer in Havana, the Cuban capital. See Page 10 for the full story

Hamilton, Bermuda  Friday, September 25, 2009

**Eddie would like to extend his deepest appreciation to saxophonist, Liset Saroza Manso, for being so versatile and musical. 'Indeed, her contribution to our Cultural Exchange Recital in August, 2009, at the Casa de la Cultura de La Plaza, resulted in being a very stimulating musical experience for all of my Bermudian students.'**

# El Centro Nacional de Escuelas de Arte de Cuba

## El Centro Nacional de Escuelas de Arte de Cuba

se complace en presentar su programa invernal de percusión y jazz conducido por el profesor bermudense

### EDDIE MING

Acompañado por Lina Liset Saroza Manso (saxofón)

Auspiciado por la Escuela Nacional de Música de Cuba y el SABIAN CYMBAL MAKERS de New Brunswick, Canadá

Tendrá lugar desde el 30 de noviembre al 8 de diciembre 2009 en el
CNEART
de 1:00 pm a 3:00 pm

Para más información puede llamar al CNEART al teléfono 202-2326 ext. 122

Patrocinado por Sabian Cymbal Makers, Rythm LAV Bermudas y el Memorándum de Entedimiento Cultural entre Cuba y Las Bermuas

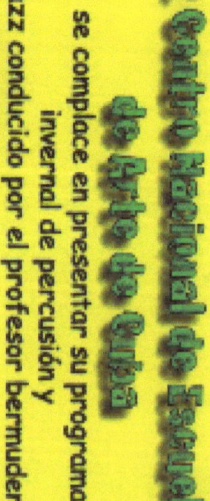

sabian.com

**Eddie was Bermuda's representative for Havana's 25th International Jazz Festival 2009, which featured Bermuda's # 1 band : 'THE UNIT.'**

**Eddie at Cuba's Hotel Riviera, 2009.**

# ORCHESTRATING IDEAS
## *IDEAS ORQUESTRALES*

Any basic exercise will give you a place to begin building your personal orchestrating possibilities:

*Cualquier ejercicio de base le dará una idea donde comenzar a construir sus posibilidades personales orquestar:*

Given exercise:
*Ejercicio:*

Examples:
*Ejemplos:*

These are just three possibilities to build on.

*Estos son sólo tres posibilidades para construer.*

**The proceeding duet G was created from the same concept.**

*El dúo procedimiento G fue creado a partir del mismo concepto.*

# Eighth and Sixteenth Note Combinations

## *Combinaciones de Corchea y Semicorchea*

These combinations were created from orchestrating pages 24 through 28 in 'Ted Reed's Syncopation Drum Book.'

*Estas combinaciones fueron creados a partir de la orquestación a través de las páginas 24 a 28 en el libro "Syncopation" de Ted Reed.*

The combinations are endless:     *Las combinaciones son infinitas:*

2 Bar example:     *2 compas de ejemplo:*

Written:     *Escrito:*

Played:     *Tocado:*

**Take note** that in the second bar, an accent is employed to give this two measure exercise a new idea, with added expression and substance. When the proper feel has been fully developed, the student should experiment with the example given, exploring the use of the accent, by creating his or her own patterns of accents, until he or she becomes an expert on this given subject.

***Tomar nota*** *de que en el segundo compá un acento se emplea para dar a esta medida dos ejercicios una nueva idea, con la expresión y el contenido añadido. Cuando el buen olfato que se ha desarrollado plenamente, el estudiante debe experimentar con el ejemplo dado, explorando el uso del acento, mediante la creación de sus propios patrones de acentos, hasta que él o ella se convierte en un experto en este tema dado.*

**The Royal Gazette**

CELEBRATING BERMUDA'S 400TH ANNIVERSARY

BERMUDA, SATURDAY, OCTOBER 31, 2009

# Drum school students earn Cuban honours

**By Nadia Arandjelovic**

Drum school students ventured to the National Centre School for the Arts in Cuba and returned with renewed excitement about music.

Eddie Ming's Drum School took ten students between the ages of eight and 60 to Havana, to take part in a five-day music programme in August.

The students were presented with certificates this week by Premier Ewart Brown, who commended them for their achievement: "Let me say to you that 30 years from now when you look at your certificate and you see each other you will be talking about the time you spent in Havana.

"You have no idea how important it is that you have done this, because you have opened up doors that other Bermudians will follow in."

Continued Dr. Brown. "Ten years ago it would have been unheard of for a group of young Bermudians to be going to Cuba on a serious mission about music, so I want to congratulate and commend Mr. Ming on his insight and his vision in order to make it possible for you to go."

Chieneka Raynor, Cameron Jeffers, Kirk Wilks, Jevonie Dowling, Tarique Brown, Grace Edwards, Bryson Doers, Tajai O'Connor, Stephanie Howes and Nick Swan all travelled to Cuba. They returned to Bermuda with a more serious attitude about their craft. Said Mr. Ming: "They seem to be more eager and more excited about coming to the workshops and the rhythm lab in St. George's, so it makes my job easier in the end. That's my payback for exposing them to a new culture.

"Even if it only inspires them for one day it makes my job easier. It's an investment to make the student and teacher relationship stronger."

While in Cuba, the students met underprivileged children who used music as a way to escape their reality. The children were extremely disciplined and dedicated to their craft and some, even as young as 10, were already playing at the professional level.

Mr. Ming said: "That's the difference, that's one of the main reasons I took them there."

According to Mr. Ming, it wasn't enough to tell them about Cuba, the students had to go there themselves to see and feel the culture. Bryson, a 16-year-old CedarBridge Academy student agreed.

"It was a good experience. When I first got there I had no idea what the experience was going to be like, but I ended up falling in love with it.

"The children there are so good. They are much better than us. So I really want to go there again to learn the music."

Mr. Ming, who also teaches in several Cuban cultural schools, is hopeful the experience broadened their horizons.

He said: "I hope the kids from Bermuda really appreciated it and in the future they would learn that the only way to get on top of the instrument they are studying, or the instrument they like, is to study, to invest some serious time on it (and) to practise."

Photo by Glenn Tucker

**Well done:** Chieneka Raynor, Cameron Jeffers, Kirk Wilks, Jevonie Dowling, Tarique Brown, Grace Edwards, Bryson Doers, Tajai O'Connor, Stephanie Howes and Nick Swan all travelled to Cuba, with drummer Eddie Ming and earned ceritcates in music they were congratulated by Premier Dr. Ewart Brown yesterday on the steps of the City Hall.

# HI-HAT PROCEDURE

## *PROCEDIMIENTO DE PLATILLOS HI*

The opening and closing of the Hi-Hat has become a very important and effective voice in this particular style of drumming.

The motion for the Hi-Hat is: Toe Up, to open; and Toe Down Heel Up to close.

*La apertura y cierre de la Hi-Hat se ha convertido en una voz muy importante y eficaz en este particular estilo de tocar la batería.*

*El movimiento de la Hi-Hat es: dedo del pie para arriba, para abrir y, los dedos del pie hacia abajo, para cerrar.*

Practice examples given:                                                                                   *Practica ejemplos:*

Example 1:

*Ejemplo 1:*

Toe Up / Toe Down, Heel Up

Example 2:

*Ejemplo 2:*

Examples 1 and 2 combined with added bass drum and snare drum complete:

*Los ejemplos 1 y 2 combinados con adición de Bombo y Caja completa:*

Written:                                                                                                                       *Escrito:*

# Additional Open and Close Hi-Hat Patterns with Added Bass and Snare Drum Notes

## *Patrones Adicionales de Hi Cerrados y Abiertos*

The student should make an effort to exhaust ALL possibilities of these open and close Hi-Hat variations with added Bass and Snare drum notes.

*El estudiante debe hacer un esfuerzo para agotar todas las posibilidades de estos abrir y cerrar las variaciones de Hi-Hat con las notas de bombo y notas de caja.*

These Hi-Hat voices require perfect co-ordination and should be executed with graceful movements.

*Estas voces Hi-Hat requieren perfecta coordinación, y debería ser ejecutado con movimientos graciosos.*

Bermudian students join together, to demonstrate the principles of music, and the discipline of Ming's 'Rhythm Lab,' that made it possible for them to perform in Havana.

Pictured above are: (top) Gracie Edwards; (center) Bryson Doers; and (bottom) Tajai O'Connor.

# The History of SABIAN Cymbal Makers

I would like to start by thanking SABIAN for all of their support concerning the work that I am doing in the schools in Havana, Cuba.

The question that everyone keeps asking is, how did SABIAN get its name ? And I respond by saying that the Founder and Director, Robert Zildjian and his wife, Willi, have three children – a daughter, and two sons.

| Daughter, | Sally | = SA | |
|---|---|---|---|
| Son, | Bill | = BI | **= SABIAN** |
| Son, | Andy | = AN | |

I like to think of it as 'keeping it in the family.' ( *Eddie Ming*)

The world's leading cymbal producing factory is located on Meductic's Main Street, southern New Brunswick, Canada; and was founded in 1982.

Today, SABIAN sells seven basic series, with each type offering dozens of different models that provide dozens of sizes and tones. SABIAN produces : The B8, a Beginners' model; The B8 PRO; The PRO; The Signature Series; The AA; The AAX; and, The Hand-Hammered SABIAN - a top of the line cymbal, for the most serious and talented musicians in the business.

## La Historia de los fabricantes de platillos SABIAN

*Me gustaria empezar dando las gracias a SABIAN por todo su apoyo con respecto a la labor que estoy haciendo en las escuelas en La Habana, Cuba. La pregunta que todo el mundo no cesa de preguntar es, ¿como SABIAN su nombre? Y yo respondo diciendo que el fundador y director, Robert Zildjian y su esposa, Willi, tienen tres hijos – una hija y dos hijos.*

*hija, Sally     = SA*

*hijo, Bill      = BI*          **= SABIAN**

*hijo, Andy    = AN*

*Me gusta pensar en él como "lo mantiene en la familia." (Eddie Ming)*

*El líder mundial en la fábrica de producción de platillo se encuentra en la calle principal del Meductic, el sur de Nuevo Brunswick, Canadá, y fue fundada en 1982.*

*Hoy en día, SABIAN vende siete series de base, con cada tipo de oferta de decenas de modelos diferentes que ofrecen docenas de tamaños y tonos. El SABIAN produce: B8, modelo para principiantes; El B8 PRO; PRO; la serie Signature; la AA; El AAX, y la Batida a Mano SABIAN – un tope de linea del platillo, para los músicos más graves y con talento en el negocio.*

# 38 BONUS SOLO IDEAS

## *38 IDEAS EXTRAS DE SOLOS*

The proceeding pages presented here are mixtures of voices and figures that are quite challenging. Continue to repeat the first idea until you are completely comfortable with the phrasing before starting the next one. All eighth notes are to be played with a triplet feel.

*Las páginas de proceder se presentan aquí, son mezclas de voz y datos que son bastante difíciles. Continuar con la repetición de la primera idea hasta que esté completamente a gusto con la redacción antes de comenzar la siguiente.*

Example:

*Ejemplo:*

Here are some suggested combinations for a melodic four-bar solo:

From Section A1: Bars #1, 4, 6 and 14

Some combinations may require special attention, so keep at it and build your four-bar solo slowly. Work towards creating eight, twelve and sixteen bar solos. You will soon discover how closely related they are.

*Aquí están algunas combinaciones sugeridas para un solo melódico de cuatro compas.*

*Desde la sección A1: Compa # 1, Compa # 4, Compa # 6, y Compa # 14.*

*Algunas combinaciones pueden requerir una atención; especial, por lo que mantendrá a la misma, y construir tu solo cuatro barras poco a poco, y trabajar hacia la creación; de ocho, doce, dieciséis y solos-bar. Pronto descubrirá; cuán estrechamente relacionados que son.*

# ADDITIONAL BONUS GROOVE IDEAS

This bonus section, A2 – B2 – C2 – D2 and E2, contains a more challenging and advanced approach to these more rhythmic beats with Cymbal Bell patterns, and added Hi-Hat displacement combinations, that will give a variety of options for you to create, and the ability to express yourself well in this style.

# *IDEAS ADICIONALES DE GROOVE*

*Esta sección D2 – A2 – B2 – C2 y E2, contiene un enfoque más difícil y avanzó a estos golpes rítmicos con la copa de platillo, y añadió combinaciones Hi-Hat desplazamiento, que le dará una gran variedad de opciónes para que usted cree, y la capacidad de expresarse bien en este estilo.*

# Bonus Section A1

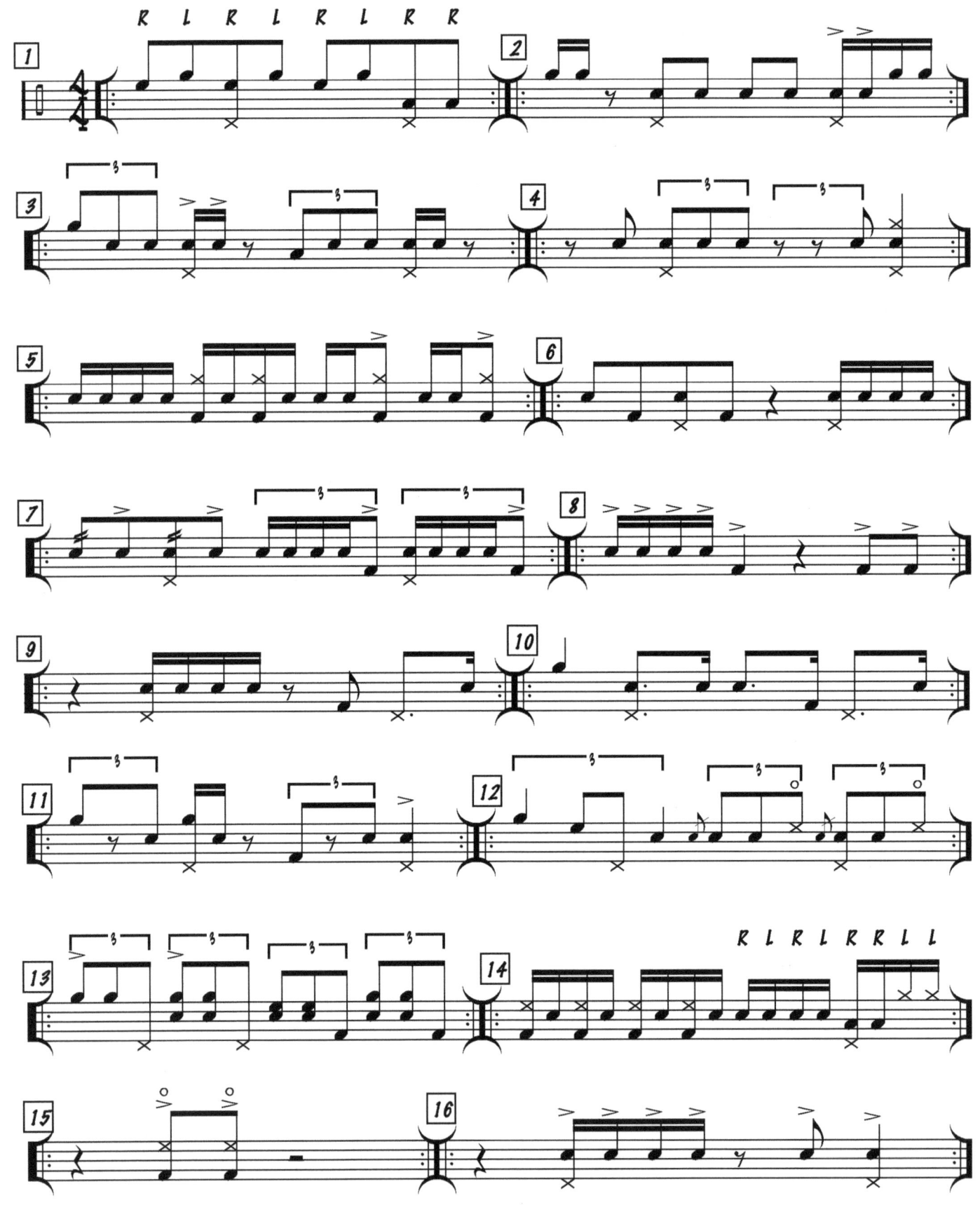

# Bonus Section B1

# Bonus Section C1

# Bonus Groove A2

# Bonus Groove B2

# Bonus Groove C2

# Bonus Groove D2

# Bonus Groove E2

# 6/8 Bonus Grooves

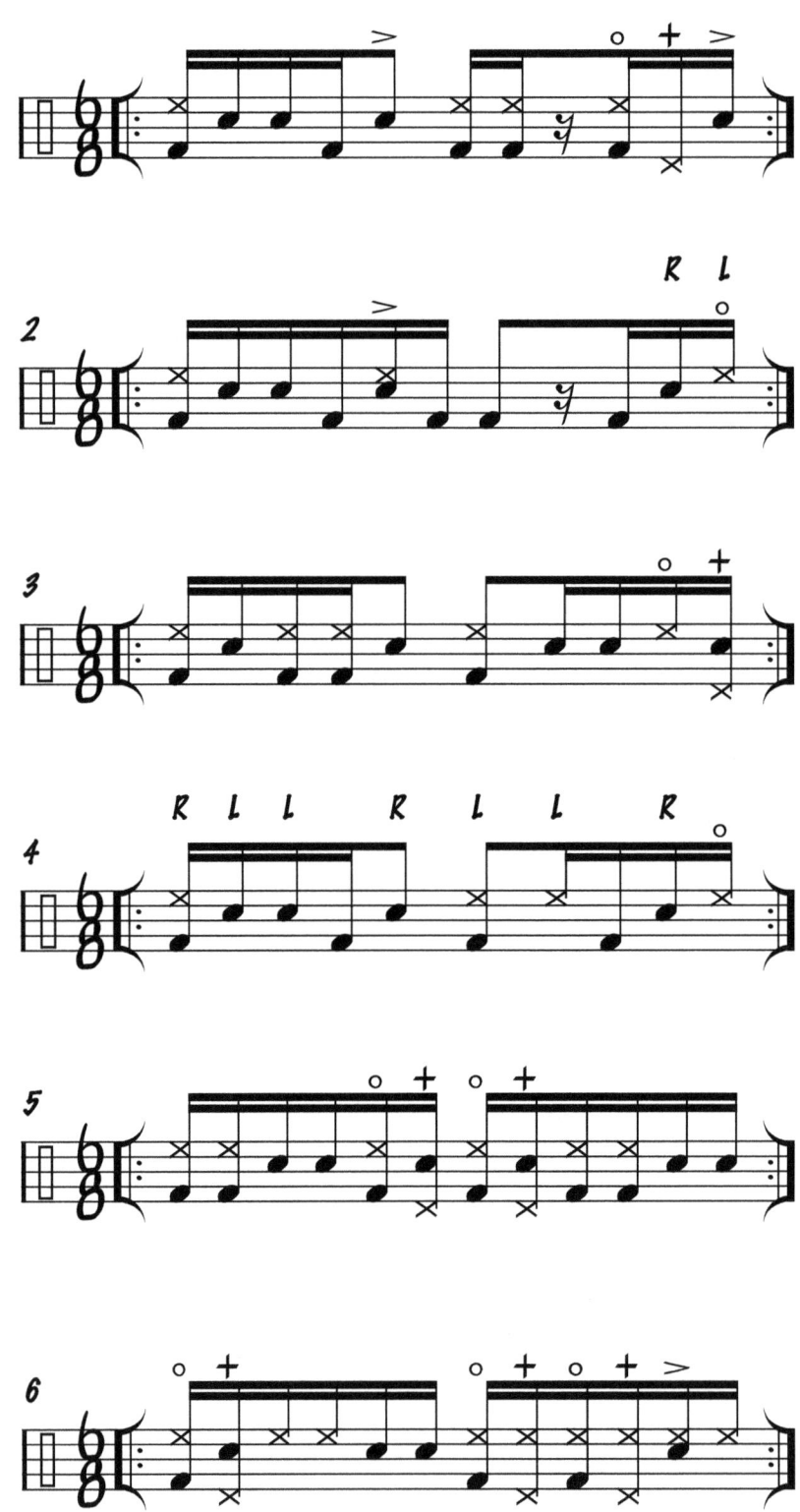

# 6/8 BONUS GROOVES

### on the proceeding page

Presented on the following page, are 6 additional grooves with open and close Hi-Hat patterns. The student will find these grooves to be an excellent practice source in 6/8, which will offset any difficulties he or she might have later on. And, in the event that you are called upon to play a Fusion 6/8 Groove, you might feel awkward compared to the previous grooves in 4/4……..the more you review and practice, the more natural these grooves will become.

# *GROOVES EXTRAS 6/8*

### *en la pagina de proceder*

*Se presentan 6 grooves adicionales con los patrones de Hi-Hat abrir y cerrar. El alumno encontrará estas grooves para ser una fuente práctica excelente en 6/8, que compensarán las dificultades que él o ella podría tener más adelante, y en caso de que están llamados a desempeñar una fusion 6/8 groove. Pueden sentirse incómoda en comparación con las grooves anterior en 4/4. El examen de la que más y la práctica, la más natural que se convertirá.*

# ESSENTIAL SNARE DRUM EXERCISES
## PAGES A & B

The objective of these exercises is to stimulate and motivate one's desire to become the best that one can be. By perfecting these exercises, one's reading skills will be elevated.

**NOTES:**

The advantage of becoming an accomplished sight reader will be rewarding, and will allow the individual to have the ability to access all forms of music, thereby achieving an incredible amount of knowledge if he or she so wishes.

# *EJERCICIOS ESENCIALES DE CAJA*
## *PÁGINAS A Y B*

*El objetivo de estos ejercicios es estimular y motivar el deseo de convertirse en el mejor. Al perfeccionar estos ejercicios, las habilidades de lectura se desarrollan.*

***NOTAS:***

*La ventaja de convertirse en un consumado lector a primera vista será gratificante y permitirá al individuo tener habilidad para acceder a todas las formas de música, por tanto lograr una cantidad increíblede conocimiento si así lo desea.*

# Snare Drum Exercise A

# Snare Drum Exercise B

# JAZZ STUDIES

The proceeding six pages: **J** 1, **J** 2, and **J** 3, in 4/4 Jazz, and pages **J** 4, **J** 5, and **J** 6, in 3/4 Jazz, all contain musical phrases that display all four elements that can be applied when performing with a Jazz Ensemble.

**NOTES:**

Keeping in mind that your Ride Cymbal, Stick height and its 'area of attack' must always remain the same at all times; making your Ride Cymbal sound personal, and the Time Flow very emotional.

Having the right Stick height will make the execution much easier when incorporating the other elements.

One of the most important abilities that a drummer must demonstrate is that his role is to support the Ensemble by keeping steady time.

# *ESTUDIOS DE JAZZ*

*Las siguientes seis páginas: J 1, J 2 y J 3 en Jazz 4/4 y páginas J 4, J 5 y J 6 en Jazz 3/4. Todas contienen frases musicales que muestran los cuatro elementos que pueden aplicarse cuando se actúa con un conjunto de jazz.*

***NOTAS:***

*Tener presente que tu címbalo, la altura de la baqueta y su "area de ataque" siempre debe ser la misma en todo momento; hacer que tu címbalo suene personal y que el flujo de tiempo suene emotivo.*

*Tener la adecuada altura de la baqueta hará la ejecución más fácil al incorporar los otros elementos.*

*Una de las habilidades más importantes que un baterista debe mostrar es su papel al apoyar la banda manteniendo el tiempo estable.*

# 4/4 Jazz studies page J1

# 4/4 Jazz studies page J2

# 4/4 Jazz studies page J3

# RIDE CYMBAL VARIATIONS

For additional study, anyone of these 4/4 ride cymbal variations with four feather bass drum notes and the hi-hat on 2 and 4 can be applied to any one of the 4/4 Jazz studies presented on pages J1, J2, and J3.

## VARIACIONES DE CÍMBALOS

Para el estudio adicional se puede aplicar a cualquiera de los estudios de jazz 4/4 presentados en las páginas J1, J2, y J3, una de estas variaciones de címbalo 4/4 con cuatro notas ligeras para el bombo y el Hi en 2 y 4.

**4/4 Ride Cymbal Examples:**

*Ejemplos de címbalos 4/4:*

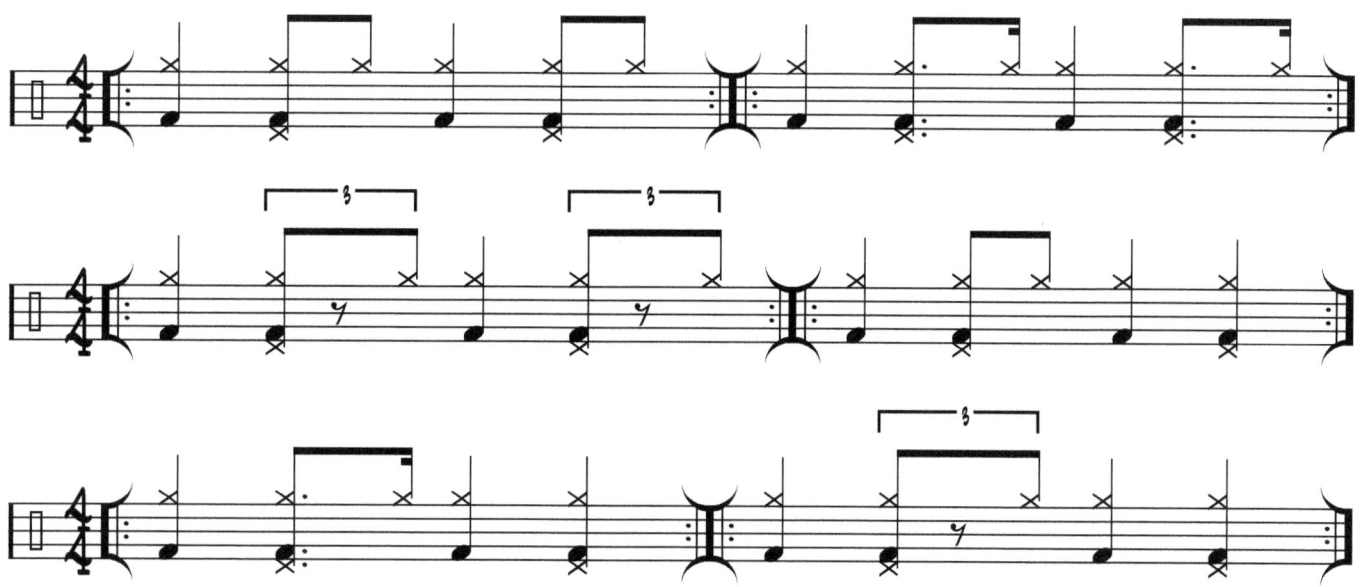

**3/4 Cymbal and Hi-Hat Examples:**

*Ejemplos de címbalo y Hi-Hat 3/4:*

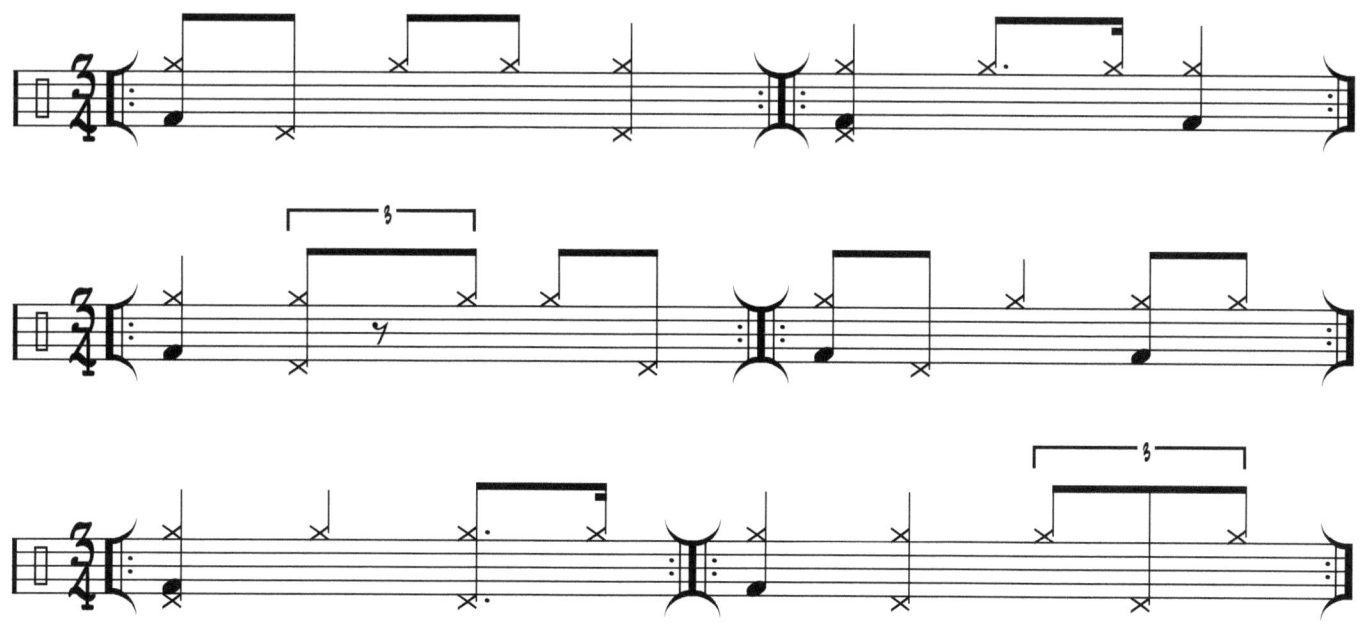

# 3/4 Jazz studies page J4

# 3/4 Jazz studies page J5

# 3/4 Jazz studies page J6

# Shifting time signatures with open and Close Hi-Hat Ideas

*Cambiando el compás con ideas sobre platillos Hi-Hat abiertos y cerrados.*

As a reminder, count when practicing these ideas to make certain that you are executing them exactly the way they are written.

*Como un recordatorio, se debe contar al practicar estas ideas para asegurarse de que se ejecuten exactamnete de la forma en que estan escritas.*

Play close attention to the heel and the toe motion of the Hi-Hat foot, making sure that the Time is locked in.

The key is to stay relaxed.

*Preste atención al movimiento del talón y el dedo gordo del pie del Hi-Hat, asegurándose de que el tiempo esté "cerrado" (preciso).*

*La clave es mantenerse relajado*

# Additional Shifting Time Signatures with Open and Close Hi-Hat Ideas

*Ideas adicionales para cambiar el compás con Hi-Hat abierto y cerrado*

When this subject has been completely mastered, then I would like to suggest that the individual try creating his or her own combinations. For instance, try this example for some logical ideas:

*Cuando esto haya sido completamente dominado, se sugiere que el individuo intente crear sus propias combinaciones. Intente este ejemplo para algunas ideas lógicas:*

And for additional study, anyone of these 3/4 ride cymbal with hi-hat variations can be applied to any one of the 3/4 Jazz studies presented on pages J4, J5 and J6.

*Y para estudio adicional, cualquiera de estas variaciones de címbalo 3/4 con Hi-Hat pueden aplicarse a los estudios de jazz 3/4 presentados en las páginas J4, J5 y J6.*

**NOTE:**

The more ride cymbal and hi-hat variations that you study, the more control and freedom you will develop.

***NOTA:***

*Mientras más variaciones de címbalo y Hi se estudien, más control y libertad se desarrollarán.*

# JAZZ PHRASES FOR BRUSHES

The object of these five two-measure phrases presented here,
is to motivate the individual to become more creative with brushes.

## *FRASES DE JAZZ PARA ESCOBILLAS*

*El objetivo de estas 5 frases de 2 compases presentadas aquí,
es motivar al individuo a ser mas creativo con las escobillas.*

**Note:**

Practice with a metronome, and experiment with different tempo settings. When you find the right tempo, work toward perfecting these phrases, and Developing the perfect feel for Jazz. These phrases sound more musical at a medium tempo - but it's your choice.

**Nota:**

*Practique con el metrónomo y experimente con diferentes configuraciones de tiempo. Cuando encuentre el tiempo adecuado, trabaje hacia el perfeccionamiento de esas frases y desarrolle sentimiento perfecto para el Jazz. Estas frases suenan mas musicales a un tiempo medio, aunque usted decide.*

Friday, July 9th 2010

Montreal's

KoSa Centre des Arts

proudly presents

Prof. Eddie Ming's Percussion Trio

BOJO

With special guests,

Bryson Doers & Tajai O'Connor

Theme entitled : CALCULATIONS

Theme Description :

Blending Dominican rhythms with Funk,

to create new ideas

that reflect strength and enthusiasm.

# KOSA

*viernes, 9 de Julio del 2010*

*El centro de artes KoSa de Montreal*

*presenta*

*El trío percusionista del Prof. Eddie Ming*

*"BOJO"*

*Con invitados especiales*

*Bryson Doers y Tajai O'Connor*

*Tema: Cálculos*

*Objetivo:*

*Mezclar los ritmos Dominicanos con la música de tipo Funk*

*para crear nuevas ideas*

*que reflejan fuerza y pasión.*

This text is dedicated to all the students that I had the opportunity to teach at

the National School of Music ( Escuela Nacional de Música ) in Cuba.

I sincerely hope that they all continue to explore every musical possibility, and to let their

imaginations dominate their limitations.

I would also like to thank

musical director, Miriam Bango and her faculty; and Amalia Garcia and her administrative staff,

for sharing some of the best days of my life.

May God continue to bless us all.

*Este texto esta dedicado a todos los estudiantes que he tenido la oportunidad de enseñar*

*en la Escuela Nacional de Música en Cuba.*

*Espero sinceramente que todos ellos continuan explorando todas las posibilidades musicales y*

*dejar que su imaginación domine sus limitaciónes.*

*También me gustaría dar las gracias a Miriam Bango, director musical y su facultad; y Amalia*

*Garcia y su personal administrativo para compartir algunas de los mejores días de mi vida*

*Que Dios siga bendiciendo a todos nosotros.*

Professor Ming

**Eddie's Bermudian students in Cuba, at his 2009 Music and Percussion Cultural Exchange Program which took place at the Escuela Nacional de Música de Cuba.**

Cameron Jeffers                    Kirk Wilks

Javoni Swan                        Chiemeka Raynor

Tariq Brown

# HISTORY OF LA ESCUELA NACIONAL DE MÚSICA

In 1962, the National Art School was founded in Cuba. It was born out of all the artistic traditions that had been the creative practice of Cuban teachers and artists for centuries. Its significance as a product of the Cuban Revolution, is the prestige that it has brought to Cuban art and culture.

Thus, the ENA or Escuela Nacional de Arte was formed. It was a multidisciplinary centre where Ballet, Music (creating The National School of Music/La Escuela Nacional de Música), Drama, Visual Arts and Modern and Folk Dance were taught at middle level, culminating in university level at the Superior Institute For The Arts (ISA).

With the establishment of the National Art School in 1962, music was the subject that most students chose to study. Young people from all over the country came to the National School of Music with the purpose of becoming capable professionals in different musical skills. In the years following the establishment of a National School of Music, and the development of music education, it became necessary to implement an intense program of study.

In 1974, with the help and collaboration of educators and specialists from the Soviet Union, the re-organization of art education in Cuba took place on a national scale, and brought about consistency in the plans and curricula of the different arts. Three levels of teaching music were established : elementary; middle; and high and advanced studies (university graduate and postgraduate levels at the Superior Institute For The Arts/Insituto Superior de Arte or ISA), as well as the division of the elementary level, in accordance with the music skills of the students. The twenty-six music programs studied in school are proceeded by seven years for long term careers (piano, violin, viola, and cello), and four years for short term careers (all other instruments). The curriculum for the four years of middle level provides the graduates with the following skills: Instrumental, Theory, and Choral Conducting. The National School of Music has helped to raise the level of music education in all the provinces of Cuba, and provides various institutions within the country for graduates of different musical skills.

The Escuela Nacional de Arte (ENA) or National School of Music plays an essential role in the preservation of Cuban culture and national identity. Today, the multidisciplinary art complex, of which the National School of Music is a part of, is responsible for producing the majority of professional Cuban artists, as well as the art and culture of the country. The National School of Music holds the medal for its range and exhibition of Cuban culture. Since its establishment, this centre has had a prestigious faculty comprising of professionals and avant-garde artists, who have played a significant part in music education in Cuba. The National School of Music has participated in national and international competitions, and has been the winner of important accolades along the way.

# HISTORÍA DE LA ESCUELA NACIONAL DE MÚSICA

*Centro Nacional de Escuelas de Arte :*

*La fundación de la Escuela Nacional de Arte en 1962 dio inicio a la extraordinaria expansión artistica, como una de las obras más trascendentales y hermosas de la Revolución Cubana expresada en el desarrollo y prestigio alcanzado por el arte en Cuba.*

*En marzo de 1962, a partir de un estudio general sobre la enseñanza artistica se ve la posibilidad de crear un centro multidisciplinario donde se encontraran las artes y donde hubiera una vinculación entre los alumnus de todas las ramas artísticas. Así se crea la Escuela Nacional de Arte (ENA). En la misma se constituirían cuatro especialidades : Ballet, Música, Arte Dramático y Artes Plásticas. Tres años después en 1965 comenzaría la enseñanza de la Danza Moderna y Folclórica.*

*Al crearse en 1962 la Escuela Nacional de Arte, la rama que a grupó mayor número de alumnus fue la de Música : jóvenes de todas partes del país llegaron a la ENA con el propósito de hacerse profesionales capaces en las diferentes especialidades. En los años siguientes el desarrollo de los estudios musicales adquirió un ritmo vertiginoso.*

*En 1974, se establecieron 3 niveles de enseñanza de la música : elemental, medio superior y superior en el Instituto Superior de Arte, así como la division del nivel elemental de acuerdo con las especialidades. Las 26 especializaciones que se estudian en la escuela, están precedidas de 7 años para carreras largas (piano, violín, viola y violoncello) y 4 años por las carreras cortas (restantes instrumentos). Los 4 años de nivel medio superior cuentan con un plan de estudios que ofrece a los graduados los siguientes perfiles: instrumentistas, teóricos y dirección coral.*

*La Escuela Nacional de Música ha contribuido a elevar el nivel de la pedagogía musical en todas las provincias y brinda la posibilidad de nutrir las instituciones del país con egresados en las diferentes especializaciones. Contribuye un aporte esencial a la Cultura Cubana la preservación del acervo musical y nuestra identidad patria. La Escuela Nacional de Música ostenta la Medalla por la Cultura Cubana. Desde su creación, este centro ha contado con un claustro estable integrado por prestigiosos especialistas y artistas de la vanguardia, quienes marcaron una pauta significativa en el quehacer pedagógico musical. La escuela ha participado en Concursos Nacionales e Internacionales, obteniendo importantes lauros, pudiendo mencionar algunos de ellos.*

*(Español)*
**Reseña del libro**
*"Batería Tradicional, Grooves Clásicos y Rellenos para Recitales del Laboratorio de Ritmos"*
*del autor y profesor bermudeño Eddie Ming,*
**por Agustin Gómez Lavín,** *professor de percusión del Conservatorio "Amadeo Roldán y el Instituto Superior de Arte, Havana, Cuba.*

*La extensa práctica como profesor e intéprete del maestro Eddie Ming brinda a los estudiantes de percusión la noción de patrones y ritmos internacionales de forma eficaz, musical y didáctica. El libro abarca piezas de los ritmos Funk, Rock, y Rhythm and Blues que contribuyen eficazmente al aprendizaje de estos ritmos internacionales. Esto constituye un desafío para los estudiantes cubanos por la posibilidad que les ofrece de ponerse en contacto con nuevos estilos musicales. Este libro contiene material extra interesante que amplía y profundiza en la aplicación de la batería tradicional en los propios grooves y rellenos que ofrece. Por tales razones, es un valioso libro de consulta para estudiantes y profesores de percusión.*

**(English)**
**Book Review** of Bermudian author and professor, Eddie Ming's
**"The Rhythm Lab's Traditional Drum Set Classic Grooves and Fills For Recitals"**
**by Agustin Gómez Lavín,** professor of percussion at the Conservatory "Amadeo Roldán," and the University For The Arts, Havana, Cuba.

**With an enormous amount of experience behind him, professor and musician, Eddie Ming, presents percussion students with an understanding of international patterns and rhythms in an efficient, musical and instructive way, which contributes to their comprehensive learning. This book covers Funk, Rock, and Rhythm and Blues, and is a challenge for Cuban students, for the possibility that it offers them to get in contact with new musical styles. The book contains an interesting bonus material, which widens and goes deeper into the application of the traditional drum set in the very same grooves and fills that it provides. For all these reasons, this is a valuable book to be consulted and used by percussion students and teachers.**

# Music Schools in Cuba where Bermudian author & professor, EDDIE MING, has taught:-

Escuela Elemental de Música, "Alejandro García Caturla"
*The Alejandro García Caturla Elementary School of Music*

Escuela Elemental de Música "Manuel Saumell"
*The Manuel Saumell Elementary Music Academy*

Escuela Elemental y Conservatorio de Música "Guillermo Tomás"
*The Guillermo Tomás Elementary School and Conservatory of Music*

Escuela Nacional de Música
*The National School of Music of Cuba*

Conservatorio "Amadeo Roldán
*The Amadeo Roldán Conservatory*

Conservatorio "Carlos Hidalgo Díaz"
*The Carlos Hidalgo Díaz Conservatory*

Escuela Vocacional de Arte "Pedro Raúl Sánchez"
*The Pedro Raúl Sánchez Vocational School of Art*

Escuela Provincial de Arte "Eduardo Abela Villareal"
*The Eduardo Abela Villareal Provincial School of Art*

ISA
*The University of Arts of Cuba*

Escuela Vocacional de Arte "Alfonso Pérez Isaac"
*The Alfonso Pérez Isaac Vocational School of Art*

Escuela Elemental de Música "Paulita Concepción"
*The Paulita Concepción Elementary School of Music*

# Introducing
# Three RHYTHM LAB Books For Drum Set
## *by Eddie Ming*

ISBN 978-0-9569878-0-8

### TRADITIONAL DRUM SET CLASSIC GROOVES & FILLS FOR RECITALS

*This book will help to prepare the student for the development of technical reading and musical fills for this particular style.*

ISBN 9781535325844

### ARTISTIC ORCHESTRATED APPLICATIONS FOR DRUM SET

*This book provides 38 Bonus Solo Ideas and 6/8 Bonus Grooves that should be explored. For the intermediate performer.*

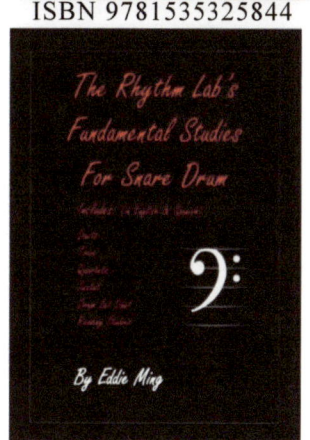

ISBN 9781519238269

### FUNDAMENTAL STUDIES FOR SNARE DRUM

*For the young ones who are enthusiastic about developing their reading skills.*

# Presentando
# Tres libres Para Batería
# Del LABORATORIO DE RITMO
# por Eddie Ming

ISBN 978-0-9569878-0-8

## RELLENOS Y PATRONES CLÁSICOS DE BATERÍA TRADICIONAL PARA RECITALES

Este libro ayudará a preparar al estudiante Para el desarrollo de lecturas técnicas y rellenos musicales, para este estilo en particular.

ISBN 9781535325844

## APLICACIONES ARTÍSTICAS ORQUESTADAS PARA BATERÍA

Para el estudiante de nivel medio y también para profesores que quieran mejorar sus habilidades creativas.

ISBN 9781519238269

## ESTUDIOS FUNDAMENTALES DE CAJA

Para los jóvenes que están muy entusiasmados con el desarollo de sus habilidades de lectura.

www.ingramcontent.com/pod-product-compliance
Lightning Source LLC
Chambersburg PA
CBHW040053160426
43192CB00002B/53